123

written by Lesley Clark
illustrated by Mark Airs

1

one teddy bear

This book belongs to:

_____

This book contributes to your child's early understanding of numbers and counting.

As you read together, help your child to say the number and trace over the number shape with a finger. Encourage her to touch and count everyday objects and, if possible, move the objects around and touch and count them again.

Try making numbers from play dough. Finally, bring counting into your conversations: "Let's go down the stairs now, one, two, three!" "How many bricks do we need to build this house? Let's count them!"

A catalogue record for this book is available from the British Library

Published by Ladybird Books Ltd
80 Strand, London, WC2R 0RL
A Penguin Company

034
© LADYBIRD BOOKS LTD MMVIII
LADYBIRD and the device of a Ladybird are trademarks of Ladybird Books Ltd

ISBN: 978-1-84646-814-8

Printed in China

2

two cars

3

three giraffes

4

four fish

5
five kites

6

six flowers

7

seven snails

8

eight ladybirds

9

nine boats

10

ten ducks

The dolls are having a tea party.

How many apples are there?

How many dolls are there?

These clothes are drying on the washing line.

How many t-shirts are there?

How many skirts?

Each of these boxes has three
butterflies.

Can you count them?

How many drinks are there?

Is there a straw for each drink?

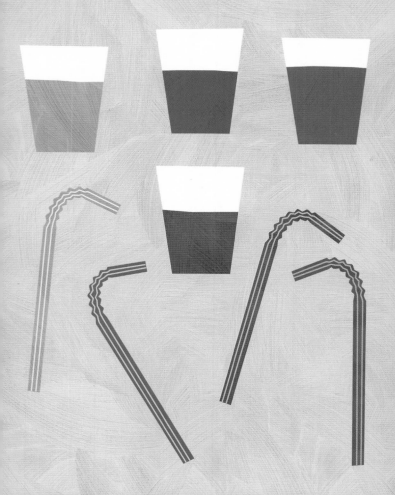

How many horses are on the farm?
How many cows?
How many pigs?

Count up all the animals and say
how many there are altogether.

How many toys are on the chair?

How many are on the floor?

How many balls are there?

Which is the largest?

Which is the smallest?